Worlds
TO IMAGINE

Dream Journeys for
Romantic Travelers

BY PETER GUTTMAN

FODOR'S TRAVEL PUBLICATIONS, INC. • NEW YORK • TORONTO • LONDON • SYDNEY • AUCKLAND • WWW.FODORS.COM

The publisher gratefully acknowledges Peter
Guttman's contribution to the development of
Fodor's "To Imagine" series.

Fodor's is a registered trademark of Fodor's Travel
Publications, Inc.

Special Sales
Fodor's Travel Publications are available at special
discounts for bulk purchases for sales promotions or
premiums. Special editions, including personalized
covers, excerpts of existing guides, and corporate
imprints, can be created in large quantities for special
needs. For more information, contact your local book-
seller or Special Markets, Fodor's Travel Publications,
201 E. 50th Street, New York, NY 10022. Inquiries from
Canada should be directed to your local Canadian book-
seller or sent to Random House of Canada, Ltd.,
Marketing Dept., 2775 Matheson Boulevard East,
Mississauga, Ontario L4W 4P7. Inquiries from the United
Kingdom should be sent to Fodor's Travel Publications,
20 Vauxhall Bridge Road, London, England SW1V 2SA.

ISBN 0-679-00024-0
First Edition

PRINTED IN THE UNITED STATES OF AMERICA
10 9 8 7 6 5 4 3 2 1

Library of Congress Cataloging-in-Publication Data
Guttman, Peter, 1954–
Worlds to imagine: dream journeys for romantic travelers /
by Peter Guttman.—1st ed.
p. cm.
ISBN 0-679-00024-0 (alk. paper)
1. Travel. I. Title.
G153.4.G88   1998
910'.2'02—dc21   98-31019   CIP

While every care has been taken to ensure the accuracy
of the information in this guide, time brings change, and
consequently, the publisher cannot accept responsibility
for errors that may occur. Call ahead to verify prices and
other information.

Readers should also remember that adventure travel and
outdoor vacations may entail certain risks. While outfitters,
trip operators, and tour guides mentioned in this book
have been carefully selected, the publisher makes no
warranties regarding their competence, reliability, and
safety practices and disavows all responsibility for injury,
death, loss, or property damage that may arise from
participation in their trips.

Acknowledgments
The immense blessing of Lori Greene's awesome spirit
and passionate support is priceless.

Huge kudos go to Fabrizio La Rocca for his splendid
insight and disciplined creativity.

Credits
Fabrizio La Rocca, Editor and Creative Director
Paula Consolo, Text Editor
Tigist Getachew, Designer
Helayne Schiff, Editorial Contributor

Globally dedicated to all my loving family, caring friends, and inspiring travel companions, who have endowed my life with their steadying embrace on this crazy, ever-spinning planet.

CONTENTS

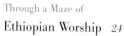

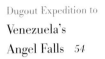

*an easy-to-use resource with essential
information for each adventure*

Imagine a lifelong honeymoon with the world you live in. Instead of lusting in frustration over seductive postcards and come-ons splashed across the pages of travel magazines, set a firm date for a new fling and give your desktop globe a spin. The whirling colors snap into focus as you touch the shaded outlines of a faraway country. Your fingertip explores those boundaries, defining remote regions where in real life a sensual, dreamlike world is in full swing.
The crossroads of its latitude and longitude begin to pinpoint your wanderlust, and you succumb to a brand-new courtship.

The unmistakable allure of a global journey can engage you in a newlywed's excitement. As you leave the airport, it becomes so easy to turn susceptible to the novel charms of fresh encounters. You're mesmerized by the rhythmic babble of an unknown language, you sniff wistfully at the puzzling aromas that perfume your path, and you're eager to sample dazzling markets where your taste buds will bloom, stimulated by uncharted flavors.

I suppose my own incorrigible passion for a kaleidoscope of stimuli was ignited decades ago, when my grandparents chaperoned this spellbound ten-year-old on scores of visits to the New York World's Fair, a showcase of Crayola hues, strangely foreign pavilions, and oddly orchestrated music—acres bursting in a dizzying nonstop carnival of happenings. Perhaps it was then that I became awestruck by the simultaneity of life's endless offerings. It now thrills me to my core to know that at the exact moment a sarong-clad, bronze-skinned duckkeeper marches his chicks in single file through the morning mist of Bali's sculpted rice paddies, blond children in a Swiss mountaintop hamlet are being tucked into bed to the soothing music of a parental bedtime story. I'm amazed that at precisely the same time a satisfied snorkeler slathers suntan lotion over an exhausted body for a summertime sprawl on the powdery sands of Australia's sunbaked barrier reef, a Sami reindeer herder navigates through a gentle Christmas Eve snowfall along a silent, moonlit forest path. It finally occurred to me that our daily existence unfurls entirely within the confines of a spinning, never-ending world's fair.

Twirling on its tilted axis in an eastward direction and at a jet plane's clip, earth commutes around the sun at an astonishing 50,000 miles per hour. All that motion would seem to centrifuge the cultures and inhabitants of this planetary blender into one homogenized blur. What is actually happening is that the long-predicted global village has shrunk our world and its once-insurmountable distances. As our sights become firmly fixed on e-mail and the Web, beepers and cell phones have strapped us closer together, and we find that supersonic flights and satellite imagery have brought the ends of the earth to within easy shouting distance.

Yet there remain splendid pockets of tranquil isolation, apparently immune to the swirl of the modern age. These bewitching regions, drifting sleepily in another time, conjure up a magical universe where we can lose ourselves as we plunge headlong into a new millennium.

Embracing the ineffable essence of a distant era, we peel away the centuries, and moving across time zones, find ourselves even more compelled to alter our perspective than to adjust our watch hands. As we swerve inside those unpredictable curves of our travel, serendipity has a way of plopping into our laps, and we learn as much about who we are as about where we are. By discovering our own reflection in the curious gaze of a former headhunter, we understand ourselves in a different way and through these ancient eyes gain new wisdom.

This valentine to the longing souls of romantic explorers offers up a candy-box assortment of tantalizing forays—total immersions in mythic dreamscapes, fairy-tale sojourns, and epic adventures. You'll need to be on your guard, though, against the heartbreak that can come with a wandering spirit: the earth is such an intoxicating place that it might not be long before you find yourself jealously eyeing still other worlds to imagine.

Peter Guttman
New York, 1998

Swimming with Angels in the

Polynesian
Lagoons of
Bora Bora

 Seemingly adrift in the immense expanse of French Polynesia, Bora Bora is an astonishing South Pacific paradise. Tiny motu islets are strung like pearls across a tranquil lagoon of stunning blues. Ragged bicuspids of basaltic rock anchor the mountainous center of this tropical sapphire pool, its shores laced by boardwalks of stilted bungalows that hover storklike over glassy seas. Roofed with palm leaves and perfumed by frangipani, your cottage hosts a private lanai that steps right down into a coral-sprinkled backyard. Take a morning wake-up dip and tag along with a fleeting school of damselfish. Venture onto a traditional outrigger toward an uninhabited Robinson Crusoe atoll, where coconut crabs inspect the palms and serenading ukuleles are interrupted by a trumpeting conch shell, dinner bell for an earthen-oven feast. A short sail away, the Lagoonarium provides a natural swim-through aquatic tank; rubbery manta rays nuzzle your backside, and a roiling frenzy of angelfish splash at the sky and render your diving mask a useless prop. Out farther, remove your jewelry and grab a safety line, as local divers lead you on a snorkeling safari, where ravenous black-tip reef sharks gather for a feeding. When you find yourself staring eye-to-eye with the hungry customers, keep your fingers together and be mindful not to seriously test the limits of supply and demand.

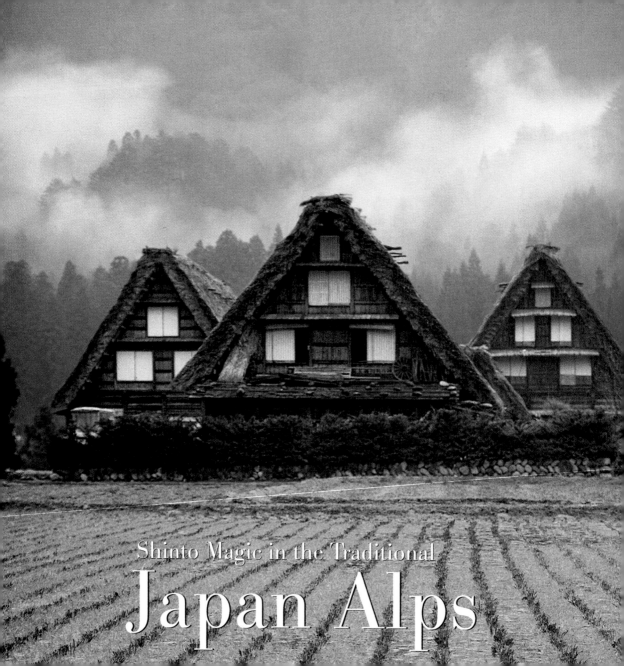

Shinto Magic in the Traditional
Japan Alps

In the hidden corners of the Japan Alps, burbling
hot springs melt snows that nourish valley cherry
trees, and quivering clouds of pink blossoms drift
away like whispered haiku on the softest April
breeze. Strolling the streets of mountain-walled
Takayama, you slip through the striped shadows of
latticework on Edo-period shop facades. Here, a
rolling thanksgiving procession of immense portable
shrines gift-wrapped in gold slowly brushes past old
teahouses and sake breweries, shoehorning through
medieval alleys to the haunting strains of plucked
shamisen. Riding high atop the festival's lantern-
strung floats, drummers catapult their bodies into a
percussive ballet, their thunderous beats
reverberating past samurai escorts that seem unrolled
from dynastic picture scrolls. Spiritual hopes are
strengthened by solemn bowing priests and by
symbolic praying hands—the rooflines of the gassho-
zukuri dominating nearby Ogimachi. In these rural
homes, sumo wrestler–size beams weightlift pitched
thatch roofing, which shelters several floors of
agricultural implements as well as worms busily
transforming a mulberry dinner into silk. On the
tatami-matted first level of your bed-and-breakfast
minshuku, don a yukata, tied at the waist, and dine
cross-legged on soybean paste grilled over magnolia
leaves. Later, warm contentedly by the open hearth,
where rising farmhouse smoke meets gentle prayers
on its journey toward the Shinto gods.

Camping with Bedouins in Jordan's
Desert Kingdom

Journey the Kings Highway and slide down a biblical time line. Trade routes of ancient tribes and caravans culminate at an enigmatic Nabataean kingdom. A canyon's narrow chink serves as trap-door entrance to the hidden metropolis of stone. Through a siq's meandering cranny of looming rock walls, you and your horse emerge onto a jaw-dropping scene. The embellished Treasury temple fills a rose-red mountain, and carved steps corkscrew up a craggy gorge to reach precipitous sacrificial altars. You survey an Ali Baba panorama of gargantuan palaces and a street of sand-castle tombs whose candy-striped interiors provide noontime respite for overheated bedouins. Stay with these nomads at nearby Wadi Ram, amidst a hauntingly lovely desertscape where afternoon mirages impound a fleet of waiting dromedaries. Taxiing toward the encampment, you buck and sway rhythmically atop your grunting lifeboat on a sea of wind-blasted sand. Below towering parapets, corduroy dunes form avenues of such immensity that your presence shrivels toward insignificance. Finally at the center of nowhere, your kaffiyeh-clad host beckons you beneath black animal-skin tents. Coffee boils over a twig fire while camel yogurt is prepared, goats are corralled, and lamb is barbecued. As dusk gilds Lawrence of Arabia's beloved stomping grounds, tuck into a sheik-worthy feast.

Sailing the Family Islands on a
Bahamas Mailboat

sliced and diced across the wharf at Potter's Cay. Find a bunk and stash your baggage aboard the *Lady Mathilda*, crammed with nervous goats, crated chickens, and sacks of anxiously awaited goods. Stowaway on an overseas postal route, in waters first explored by Columbus, as you hopscotch through a bewildering archipelago of limestone-crusted ink blots lost in the neglect of centuries. Beyond the reefs' protective bib, the ocean rudely spits its contents on deck as the captain's wheel points straight for Crooked Island. Mailboating into the Tropic of Cancer, unwind as rocking skillets of sizzling bonito clank to reggae in a ramshackle cuddy. A horn blast serves as doorbell to an approaching island, summoning a population away from domino matches and down toward the harbor. On Acklin, straw-capped aunties break from marinating chicken souse and crane their necks out of pastel cottages limned with seashells. Nearby, weathered Long Cay fishermen swap mail for their catch.

Mayaguana's Great House ruins are choked with blooming sage bushes that perfume an island so quiet you can hear the periwinkle growing. At the distant terminus of Great Inagua, vast salt pans stewing with brine shrimp attract a squadron of flamingos forming the only reliable flight pattern in this forgotten, time-warped part of the world.

Wrangle with Gauchos Across the
Pampas
of Uruguay

Tucked into an overlooked corner of the South American continent, Uruguay's forlorn heartland has for ages remained dominated by cloud-etched skies and an undulating field of dreams for the mythic gauchos. Cattle herded by the thousands move obediently across vast, treeless pampas swaying to the howling gusts of the open plains. Amidst a quilt of ranching estancias stitched together by fences that chase infinity, the colonnaded adobe-style La Calera is sequestered within a lush grove of sheltering palms. Surveying the rugged spirit of the country's timeless outback, bright-eyed cowboys framed with dark mustaches retire here for a sip of maté. You can give a hand with the chores—shear sheep, train horses, and head out into 22,000 virgin acres teeming with wild boar and nutria. Join bola-whirling wranglers attempting to regulate bovine traffic, then collect agate eroding from nearby bluffs. At the 1887 hosteria's fiery cooking pits, carnivorous appetites are satisfied by freshly culled meats carved with aplomb and served alongside vegetables collected from the huerta. As the chilly evening reveals its celestial jewelry, grab the 10-inch telescope and peek at the Southern Cross stampeding over the prairie.

Your buzzing yellow floatplane descends below a misty curtain of clouds, unveiling a panorama of pine-clad islets set amid lapis tendrils of coastline. Dropping into this scene, you spot a disheveled log raft hosting a historic Pacific Northwest lumber camp. The aircraft glides to the front dock, where you snack from trays of Dungeness crabs, snatched from their watery residence just below the Knight Inlet Lodge. The melting glaciers of nearby snowcapped peaks leak their moisture into sheets of pounding cascades that drape the sheer cliffs and pour into fjords swarming with orcas. Every autumn, armies of salmon navigate these currents, determined to trace their birthplace in upstream rivers. You board a tiny boat and motor toward these spawning grounds, where famished grizzlies line the banks and gorge themselves on a smorgasbord of fish. In a steady spray of light rain, climb the viewing decks to eavesdrop on a seemingly nonchalant clan of ursine sushi chefs filleting their meal with serrated claws. Globs of juicy roe are eyed zealously by bald eagles hovering for leftovers. Back at your evening's floating base, a hot-tub soak restores the human being among this cast of totem pole characters.

Searching for Grizzlies from

A Floating
Lumber Camp

Thermal Waters in
Dominica's Valley
of Desolation

The overwatered mountains of Dominica weep
a multitude of streaming rivers. Liana vines
wrestle the shady verdure searching for sunlight
as punch-bowl bromeliads attempt to slurp up
300 inches of yearly precipitation. The vanilla-
scented Papillote Wilderness Retreat provides
rustic haven to intrepid naturalists fired up over
the Caribbean's volcanic wonders. As peacocks
patrol this Garden of Eden, you finish a seaweed
shake and head next door to the bifurcated
cascades of Trafalgar Falls. Ease from its chilly
torrents into the soothing warmth of heated
channels, then grab your guide and begin a
cautious Dantean descent into the Valley of
Desolation. Vegetation disappears in what seems
to be the outdoor laboratory of some mad
scientist tinkering with earth's geological innards.
Through clouds of vapor, swirls of lavender and
mustard liquids spill into ravines, sopping the
inky, mineral-soaked soils. Bubbling paint pots of
mud belch a sulfuric stench across a stygian
moonscape peppered with gargling steam vents
and smoking fumaroles. In this witch's cauldron,
stay on trails to avoid breaking the fragile lava
crust and sautéing your lower limbs. An arduous
climb reveals Boiling Lake, the world's largest,
percolating in its terrestrial coffee urn. Luxuriate
behind nearby draperies of ferns, as sore muscles
are soothed in a grotto's natural Jacuzzi.

Through a Maze of
Ethiopian Worship

Hobbling out of the Abyssinian wilderness as if off the parchment of an illuminated Bible, ascetics cloaked in white robes and a haze of frankincense converge on the mystically hallowed trenches of Lalibela. Join their descent underground to a bewildering mecca of eleven Ethiopian Orthodox churches nestled in rock cradles along a labyrinthine excavation of passageways. Near Selassie Chapel, pious supplicants kiss stone portals and meander intently through passages and cavities like the residents of an ant farm. As shafts of light pierce an earthen basilica, processional crosses glimmer in the hands of gaunt priests silhouetted at the door. Listen as their whispers reveal movable stone slabs guarding the mummies of monks. Shined by centuries of naked African feet, mud boulevards and chiseled clefts reverberate with incantations that multiply into a frenzied din of ululating congregants, clinking cisterns, and thumping ox-skin drums. A bit more than a hundred miles away, in the ancient playground of the Queen of Sheba, is mythic Lake Tana, freckled with island monasteries. It is here that the Blue Nile originates, spilling from the lakeshore and tumbling in foamy swells through steep gorges. To reach its raging falls, ferry like Moses across a gentle stretch in a papyrus craft lashed with reeds, then wander briefly through the desertscape and listen for thundering sounds from above.

High above the snaking Urubamba, along dizzying slopes of orchid-studded forest, a string of footpaths reveals the hidden spirit of the Sacred Valley. In Ollantaytambo, where villainous conquistadors hit a fierce human roadblock, grain-laden llamas now double-park for manta-clad Quechuans. You hire a porter for your jaunt on the historic Inca Trail, with its 12,000-foot passes linking traces of a defunct civilization. Chewing coca leaves helps relieve altitude sickness as you clamber across log bridges and vertiginous escarpments slicked with drizzle. Peer across stacks of spiky mountains dipped in green velvet, and discover distant ridges speckled with stoic ruins. Just below, steps terrace the hill at Winay Wayna in graceful coliseum formation. Needle through Intipunku's stone doorway and gaze in wonderment at the splendor of Machu Picchu crowning the distant dreamscape. Drawn into the main plaza down an Andean escalator of more than a hundred flights of sheer granite steps, you enter a jigsaw-puzzle complex of temple precincts, religious niches, and mystical palaces. Ahead, a cryptic sundial signposts the heavens and forecasts the seasonal drenching of thirsty maize. After days of muddy hiking, indulge your own watering needs with a hot shower at the colonial-style Machu Picchu Hotel, a wonder in the very center of this condor-filled Incan universe.

Hiking Through the
Incan Universe

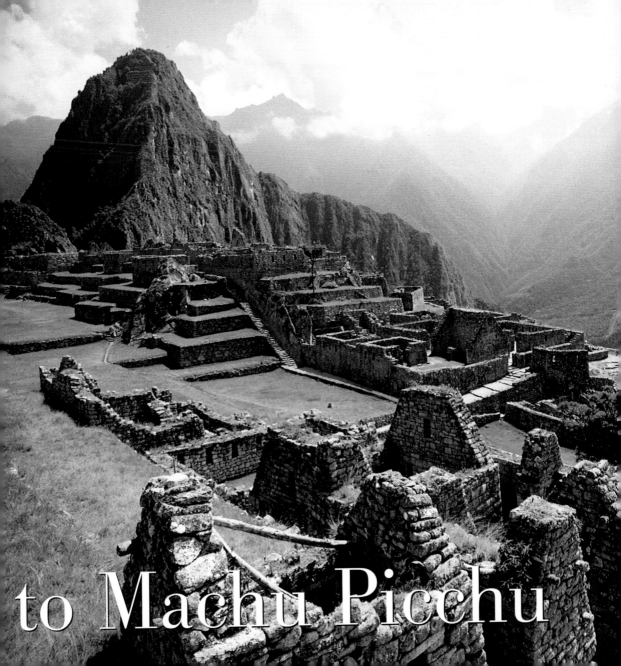

to Machu Picchu

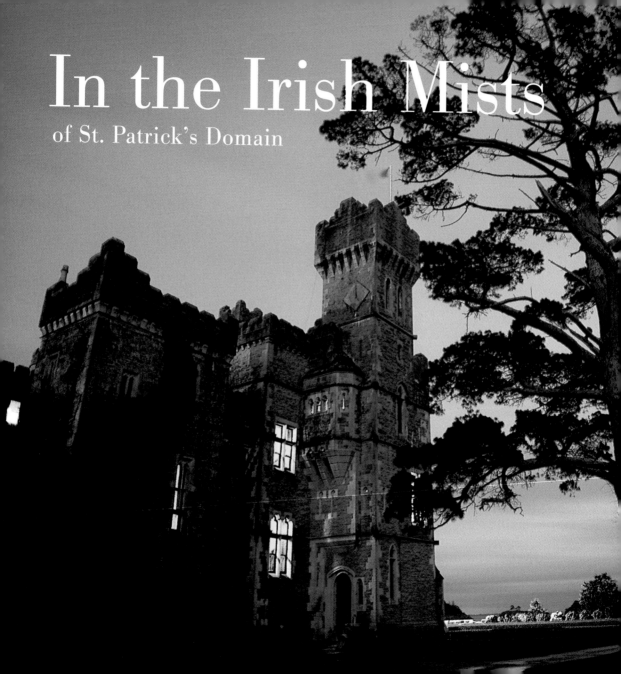

In the Irish Mists

of St. Patrick's Domain

In County Mayo's Gaelic morning mists, the lazy current of the river Cong flows through achingly lyrical sheep-flecked moorland. It dawdles by the haunted ruins of an Augustinian abbey and below the rods of tweed-capped anglers testing their bait. The waters ripple past watchtowers and under an arched stone drawbridge leading to the baronial Ashford Castle. Within, a warren of drawing rooms cloister medieval armor beneath intricately carved balustrades and paneled ceilings. The 13th-century fortress' weathered battlements and crenellated turrets are, by teatime, silhouetted in the often shy Irish sun. Splendid traps chauffeur you across the heather-scented demesne and through sunken flower gardens that fill the lakefront quadrangle. Out amongst the isles dotting Lough Corrib's mystic sheen, you cruise beneath the desolate peaks of distant Connemara and visit the remains of Inchagoill's church, founded by St. Patrick in 440 A.D. Time it just right to participate in the western world's oldest religious pilgrimage, when barefoot, shamrock-souled worshippers scramble up nearby Croagh Patrick to honor their saint on the spot where he banished the nation's snakes and fasted for forty days. Back at the chateau's inglenook, warming by the fire, you decide there's no need to challenge your own willpower, and you devour a roast rack of lamb the size of a healthy leprechaun.

Headhunter Hospitality in the

Heart of Borneo

Leave the last vestiges of modernity behind as you snuggle into a buoyant timber and glide up the pellucid current of the Skrang River. Piercing Borneo's interior, you watch a company of hornbills flee as fuzzy-headed orangutans shake the olive canopy and forage for odoriferous durian. The lush forest thickens, and you enter a twisting avenue of water that mirrors ancient condominiums for retired headhunters. Parking your dugout, you scurry up a notched log and ascend the muddy bank. Remove your shoes before entering an 800-foot-long shed roofed with thatch and perched on towering stilts tied with creeper. Inside the longhouse, a bouquet of human skulls dangles from the rafters, vacant eyes spying on Iban tribesmen, tattooed and feathered, mending fish traps and inspecting blowpipe guns. You make an offering of biscuits and fruit to the headman, then pass a column of weavers tethered to their back-strap looms, before settling on a soft mat to await juicy meats steaming in long bamboo tubes. The obligatory rice wine ferments in mammoth jars as sonorous gongs accompany the fluid movements of a paraffin lamp— lit warrior dance. Protected by mosquito netting and comforted by a conviction that the gathered scalps are but mementos of another time, you rest your weary head until awaking cockfight roosters signal the approaching dawn.

Beneath the radiant light of a tireless nighttime sun, the strongest icebreaker ever built smashes a trail to the top of the world. A floating city atomically fueled with 750,000 horsepower, the *Yamal* departs Murmansk at full gallop toward the planet's most noted piece of real estate. En route, at remote Franz Joseph Land, reconnaissance helicopters whisk you to Cape Flora, which is draped in buttercups and the rusted artifacts of less fortunate polar explorers. Nearby, your inflatable Zodiac skirts a flotilla of sharp-tusked walruses snorting angry blasts of arctic steam. At the edge of the globe's frozen skullcap, the thudding hull of this mammoth shake-and-bake nuclear reactor encounters pancake ice of delicate, crystallized lily pads. They graduate into yacht-long sheets whose fractured cobalt chunks are upended into stepping stones for marauding polar bears. A seemingly infinite turquoise and ivory finger painting stretches across an icy convex canvas. With compass-needle instincts, crowds gather on the bridge to watch the instruments tick toward 90 degrees north. Flares launch and the gangway lowers. At the point where all longitudes converge, celebrants circumnavigate the pole, dancing across every time zone and skipping over the dateline into tomorrow. Climb the radar mast to find south in all directions, and momentarily stand north of every inhabitant on earth.

To the
North Pole
by Icebreaker

Barging Bicycles Through
Holland's Tulip Playground

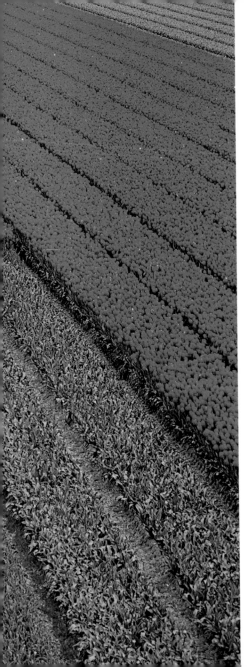

In springtime, North Holland is a scented carpet of colored geometry filling a thousand square miles of hand-built plains stolen from the seas. Guarded by an ingenious system of dikes and levees, the tile-flat polders are sliced with waterways transited by handsome barges steaming toward the Ijsselmeer coast. You bike down a boat ramp and roll into a Vermeer landscape of wildflower-matted peat meadows and bending grasslands buffeted by stiff winds. With your back as a sail, whiz toward mustard-grinding windmills that pepper the horizon, pass busy millers clomping through chores in wooden clogs, and leave behind whirling blades that seem to strain for liftoff from floral launching pads. Ding your bell to scatter wayward sheep hogging the path and dominating your view over the handlebars. Pole-driven punts and windsurfing mallards glide below, as you wheel over hump-backed swing bridges and into villages whose gabled, open-curtained homes spotlight tidy dioramas of Dutch life. Cycle through brilliant fields lit by bulbs of tulips, then head toward the narrow 12th-century streets of Alkmaar. The church square is crowded by straw-hatted porters running stretchers piled with cheeses to the weight house, but save your dairy cravings for a congenial wine and Edam cocktail hour later, aboard your bicycle-toting canal-side craft.

The Drama of a
Serengeti Safari

Surging through billows of dust, your jeep
approaches the climactic scene of an animal
kingdom's springtime drama. The Serengeti's
measureless savanna plays annual host to the
planet's largest movement of biomass. Following
thunderstorms for fresh grasses, two million
migrating wildebeests rumble across the Tanzanian
border, ignoring both customs and Kenya's drying
Masai Mara plain. Trailing along are swarms of tail-
flicking Thomson's gazelles and flighty zebras
ribboned with op-art hides. Eyeing this traveling
snack bar, a pride of lions clench limbs of acacia
while eluding clouds of tsetse flies. Pop the roof
hatch to observe drag-racing cheetahs defending
their kills from guffawing hyenas. Later, visit the
dung manyattas of the fierce Masai herders, who
subsist on a diet of blood and milk, then adjourn
to your own homey safari retreat, thankful for
the substantially finer menu. The next day, watch
giraffes gulp leaves from thorny trees, while grunts
emanate from the wrinkled snouts moisturizing
in mud-swirled hippo pools. A different overnight
at the equator's Mountain Lodge offers a more
grit-free game-viewing experience. Linger with
cocktails on your treehouse veranda as a clomping
parade of elephants and rhinos luxuriate in swampy
water holes. The salt licks are spotlit for a middle-
of-the-night audience, so be sure to place a
wake-up call to spy on the species of your choice.

Wandering
A Swiss
Fairy Tale

You'll need both hands to reach the village of Albinen, as you ascend the Leiterns, age-old ladders wedged into a cliff by ancient settlers and a thriving route for local traders in aeons past. Elsewhere, via the widespread Swiss web of mountain trails, you can descend through terraced potato fields and misty meadows into Guarda, a fairy-tale hamlet out of *Hansel and Gretel*. Pitched cobblestone lanes weave a trail toward the plazetta, fragrant with the aroma from outdoor ovens. Overburdened heifers create a symphony of tinkling cowbells as they chugalug at a handsome fountain prior to milking. Scribbled across the settlement's charming facades and on geranium-decked bay windows are lovely patterns of decorative sgraffito, an architectural signature of the Engadine. Stroll past the church square, where homework-toting bicyclists procrastinate, and just a yodel beyond, find the Hotel Meisser, created from a 1645 farmhouse and suspended 1,000 feet above the deep valley floor. A schnitzel dinner in the hay-barn dining room precedes your retirement to the manor's terrace as sunset ricochets across the Dolomites skyline.

Voodoo Culture on the
Edge of the
Amazon Basin

Rattling across a bumpy grass runway hacked through the South American forest, the Twin Otter drops you into a surprisingly different hemisphere. Suriname's unknown interior adjoins the Amazon basin yet is home to the vibrant African culture of a people who are descendants of escaped Dutch-owned slaves. Loose garments swathe an energetic crew of these Bush Negroes, who load you into hollowed tree trunk vessels for a multiday excursion to their Saramakan settlements. Portaging through churning cascades, you arrive at the tiny island village of Kumalu, where comfortable lodging awaits in traditional thatch-roofed cabins shaded by swaying palms. Wedged among the fronds, the nests of pink-toed tarantulas provide a convenient base for their moonlit forays. Just across the river, boys armed with slingshots prepare for a showdown with golden-winged parakeets intent on retrieving dispersed Kapok tree seeds. Topless women bake their laundry on shoreline rocks, as you pay respects to the Granman and then engage in a shamanistic Wasi Wi bathing ritual. Gathered from the witch doctor's jungle pharmacy, hefty bunches of medicinal herbs are pulverized into a healing brew. As the brief tropical twilight melts into darkness, hypnotic drumbeats move frenzied dancers, who sweat glistening beads of reflected bonfire. Their mesmerizing voodoo trances erupt into a barefoot strut over glowing embers of fire, burning only their indelible images into your brain.

Shrouded in mist and Romanian superstition, the horseshoe-shaped Carpathian range trembles under a cobweb of bedeviling legends. Step into this haunting land of Vlad Dracul, whose sadistic regime sparked the creation of a grisly fictional vampire. Crawl through the hidden rock stairwells of Bran Castle, a reputed clubhouse for the notorious impaler. Like many brooding citadels across Transylvania, it grips a stony outcrop. In nearby Sighisoara, a 15th-century market town, the monstrous clock tower displays intimidating medieval armor. In its shadows, at the foot of Tin Makers Street, wolf down a meal of beefsteak and cabbage at the count's birthplace. Continuing south, aim a rowboat across marshy waters toward the church at Snagov, where the earthly remains of a villainous spirit are marked by a bejeweled portrait. You might question the count's dissolution after a journey to remote Borgo Pass. En route, you'll encounter rubbernecking oxcart drivers and a chain of ancient monasteries wallpapered in comic-strip frescoes featuring ghoulish scenes of tortured sinners meeting their demise. On a hilltop, the forbidding Dracula Castle Hotel spooks overnight guests. The dungeon's candle-toting escort slowly lifts both its creaky casket and the hair on your arms. Checkout time has new meaning as you beat a hasty departure into the biting winds of a moonlit Halloween night.

Trailing in the Footsteps of
Transylvania's Dracula

Spiritual Trances in
A Balinese Paradise

A vulcanian speck in the planet's longest archipelago, Bali is Hinduism's most distant outpost. Here, slivers of graceful steps carve emerald hillsides into dramatic stadiums of rice paddies, while troops of macaques plunder sacred nutmeg forests. Lose yourself in the exuberant religious celebrations that crisscross the island's dreamy landscape. In the fields, a procession of devotees bedecked in brocade ford murmuring streams as they balance high-rise offerings of exotic fruits and patterned cakes with great cranial discipline. The tintinnabulary gongs and xylophones of a batik-capped gamelan summon animistic spirits and intone complex rhythms for Ubud's dancers. Their stylized pantomimes are as old as the Ramayana and seem to morph into shadow puppets displayed along clogged roads to Besakih. Don a sash for this holiest site, where scowling demons sculpted in lava are misted by smoldering sandalwood. These menacing gargoyles compete for your attention with the maroon smiles of a betel nut—chewing horde hell-bent on appeasing the gods. Later, when the sun sinks on another Indonesian day of cosmic harmony, you retire to your courtyarded nirvana. By a private open-sided pavilion, the garden's plunge pool invites moonlit languor and induces a firm sense of gratitude that there is indeed a heaven on earth.

The wailing muezzins summon the faithful to prayer from skinny minarets struck like candles by morn's pearly light. You slip through a keyhole-shaped gateway with an experienced guide and penetrate the mysterious, time-worn casbah of Fez. A maze of narrow lanes fills with the bustle of a medieval rush hour. Impatient souk-bound traders lead ill-tempered mules and asses burdened with vegetables, while confident merchants intoxicate potential customers with mint tea. Ahead, a vibrant potpourri of spices scents noisy bazaars. Shirtless tanners submerge hides in simmering paint-box tubs, and dyers with blood-red hands heave skeins of wool from steaming cauldrons onto sagging clotheslines. Duck through scalloped arches at an ancient Koranic school and into a perfumed courtyard swimming with dizzying Islamic patterns. The pinging bells and clanking cups of tassel-hatted water bearers offer cooling solace to heavily veiled schoolgirls racing darkness home. Dangling from the neck of a snake charmer, leery cobras point the way back through a phalanx of concerned astrologers and embellishing storytellers. Overnight at a pleasure pavilion where fountains and the dazzling rhythms of belly dancers lull you into an *Arabian Nights* trance. Munch your flaky pigeon pastilla and dine like a sultan.

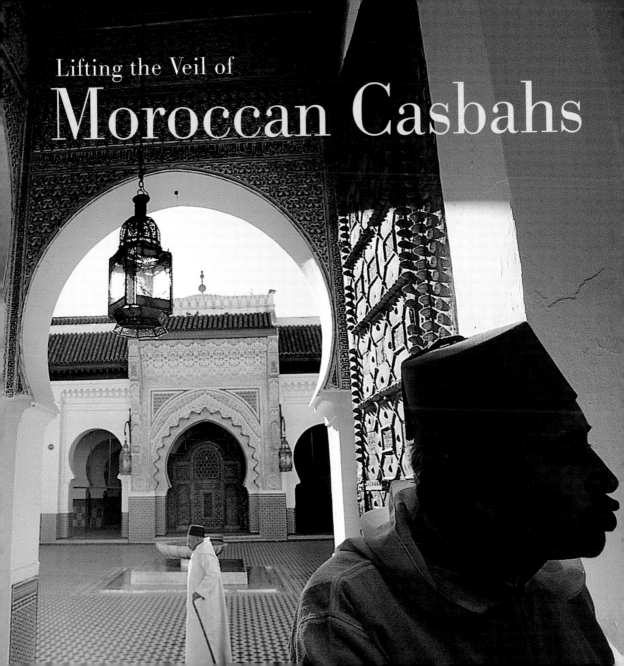

Lifting the Veil of
Moroccan Casbahs

Dugout Expedition to
Venezuela's Angel Falls

Rising from deep within the fabled shadows of Sir Arthur Conan Doyle's prehistoric *Lost World*, towering shafts of limestone stretch into the clouds, creating mysterious evolutionary islands of time high above a luxuriant savanna. Wraparound waterfalls churn the frothy Canaima Lagoon, the continuous whoosh serving as soundtrack for your cozy base camp. At the Sapo cataracts, you duck behind torrents stained tangerine by tannin from the bark of trees above. Launch a curira into the Rio Carrao and spend several days navigating this hand-carved log to the world's highest waterfall. Picnic on Orchid Island and swim across the Fountain of Happiness before distant thundershowers scatter flocks of macaws and add resistance to your upstream struggle. Hang a right up Churrin's tumultuous rapids to reach Ratoncita Island, where hammocks fill a thatched pavilion. A troupe of chattering monkeys peers through burgeoning vegetation, as flame-licked chicken is served to fatigued explorers. At daybreak hop a gurgling bridge of rocks to the base of a soaring tepui. A stubborn nimbus reluctantly parts to reveal a copper castle chiseled from the heavens and shielding a 3,000-foot bridal veil that gushes out of the firmament. Found only in 1937, Angel Falls is a cascading kilometer of free fall—a heavenly spirit in the sky.

Steaming in
Lapland's Crystal Wilderness

North of Rovaniemi and straddling the Arctic Circle, Finland's lonely fells seem etched from Christmas cards. Reindeer scamper across wintry tracts dabbed by stunted pines and dwarfed birch. Listen to the hush beneath a stained-glass sky so quiet the slightest breeze prods icicles varnishing delicate aspen fingers to play in a choir of chimes. As you grab the reins for a Santa's-eye view, your sleigh swooshes across Lapland's snowflake-dusted tundra, past scrambled ptarmigan tracks, and back toward the Sami herder's farm. Under the conical shelter of his tepeelike kota, gobble up meaty stew simmering in a flame-tickled kettle. When an umbrella of darkness slides over the creaking woods, make your way by the glow of sculpted ice lanterns to a nearby hunter's cabin and its adjoining sauna. Remove your clothes and all workweek pretensions, then ladle a wooden bucket's contents over sizzling log-fired rocks. While you sink into a tingling miasma of vapors and perspiration, slap your body with fragrant birch whisks, and feel your circulation race like an eager team of huskies. In true Nordic tradition, steamroll through the snow in your birthday suit, then watch the heavens applaud. An aurora's shimmering blanket of dancing luminescence lights your path back to the lodging's blissful embrace.

Jaunting through the winding back alleys and bazaars of Udaipur, your rickshaw dodges trudging elephants and preoccupied swamis clogging midtown traffic. Reaching opulent Shiv Niwas Palace, you peer through ornate gazebos onto glass-calm Pichola, where island castles gleam like marble water lilies under a blonde lunar beam. A floating apparition, the bone-white Lake Palace Hotel is fastened to a tiny nugget of rock, with secluded niches and an arabesque parterre of lemon-dotted lotus ponds. Built as a maharani's trysting court, this sonnet in stone flaunts cupolaed pavilions and carved terraces outside its regal suites. Duck inside, where filigreed screens veil ivory chairs, and a checkerboard of inlaid marble floors and stained glass panels reflects rays dancing offshore. Liquid riffs wept by a mournful sitar waft across a courtyard, where flocks of giant fruit bats scratch at a bloodshot moon. Throughout Rajasthan, this fully glowing disk triggers an endless stream of Hindu pilgrims who cluster annually for auspicious dips off the ghats of Pushkar's holy waters. While they swarm the village's maze of ashrams and rest houses, you are swept into this desert oasis and the world's largest camel fair. A Felliniesque riot of blazing turbans, gaudy eunuchs, and tightrope acrobats provokes a stupor that lingers well after the last dung-scented campfire is snuffed.

Rajasthani Hallucinations Across

A Maharaja

Wonderland

Seeking Mountain Tribes in
Papua New Guinea

In the rainy core of the world's second largest island, steeply corrugated ridges box in hidden valleys of Stone Age cultures, anthropological time capsules of people unknown until the past few decades. Here in Papua New Guinea's natural greenhouse, you journey through garden hamlets where fenced compounds guard taro patches and patrolling Highlanders hoist black bows made of palm and arrows tipped with human bone. Dropping in on the Huli Wigmen, you observe as they adjust their flower-decked wigs framing vividly graphic facial canvases that summon the spirit of Picasso. Their mushroom-shaped toupees are donated by crew-cut wives who tend to squealing prized pigs. Frightening apparitions, clay-coated Asaro Mud Men traverse the hills to Mount Hagen's celebratory sing-sing, where a convergence of clans blurs into a rainbow of plumage, beads, and paint, stomping to the fevered beat of lizard-skin kundus. You resort to the blossoming aerie of Ambua Lodge, a charming cluster of native-style huts on the edge of mossy woods. Vine bridges dip across gorges, where the misty film of pounding falls hangs heavy, and ostentatious birds of paradise arch gracefully over a village of their feathered incarnations playing flute in the forest below.

A Mauritian Carnival of Cultures

Basted in the world's warmest ocean, Mauritius sits at a maritime traffic circle of spice trading routes just inside the Tropic of Capricorn. Like a wedding band, a fringing coral reef creates a halo around the island, its mountainous interior formed by volcanoes now extinct. Head for the hills and immerse yourself in the mélange of exotic cultures, which sprang from the nation's commercial marriage to the sea. Through billows of rippling sugarcane, you follow a festival march of phosphorescent floats borne by the Tamil faithful, who are liberally pierced with sprays of silver needles. Foreheads punctuated only by red bindi, they lumber steadily toward the deity-studded temple. Across the valley, in the shade of a pagoda, Chinese fortune-tellers fill time slurping fried noodles shaken in roadside woks. Tossing more furiously are the shuffling hips of the erotic sega dancers embracing passion beneath the spreading arms of an ancient banyan tree. Join muscled guitarists and floral skirts swirling to an African rhythm, spun from slavery's evil roots and pounded out on the ravane's goatskin hoop. Back on the coast, relax to the softer beat of waves lapping the talcum-powder sands off the Royal Palm's sheltered lagoon. A brief catamaran sail is ample appetizer for sunset's visual banquet, as you prepare for another velvet evening in paradise.

The Icy Frontiers of
Extraterrestrial
Antarctica

Lurching through the fiercely wind-lashed waves of the Drake Passage, your snug expedition ship rollercoasters south toward the world's underbelly. Soon, snowy petrels curlicue in flight over jade icebergs drifting like frozen palaces toward a warm Atlantic meltdown. You approach the extraterrestrial monochromes of Half Moon's harbor, where broken hunks of Antarctica coalesce into ponds of fractured eggshells. A nesting colony of tuxedoed chinstraps steal pebbles as they stroll pungent slopes of slippery pink guano. Celebrate your mainland arrival at Paradise Bay with champagne, and toboggan down steep nunataks on a makeshift sled. Near Palmer Island, where drooling crabeaters dine on krill, you crawl gingerly into slippery tunnels and through a cave of shining azure. Back at sea, distant jags hint at the approaching spectacle on South Georgia. Adjust your knee-high boots and wade ashore, avoiding groaning patches of tussock grass, where molting elephant seals bathe in fog like a pile of overinflated rubber tires. Just beyond, an astonishing crowd of 100,000 screeching king penguins carpets the glaciated valley with a deafening cacophony, reminding you that we are outnumbered bit players in earth's awesome zoological theater.

Riding Malay Rails on the
Eastern and Oriental Express

Chuffing engines announce your egress from Singapore, and the shrinking island soon vanishes behind the Johor Causeway. Clacking across aging trestles, past oil palm plantations, and around serried rows of latex-oozing rubber trees, the *Eastern and Oriental Express* plunges headlong through the setting of a Somerset Maugham novel. Sybaritic dreams and the romance of the rails are boxed in twenty luxe carriages for a fortunate coterie moving through the Malay Peninsula's karst. After the morning's Thai border crossing, you disembark, then float on a motorized raft beneath the notorious bridge on the River Kwai, passing languid houseboats and log-hauling pachyderms. All aboard the train again, you wobble down corridors shaking their marquetry, past a hand-fondling, silk-robed palm reader and beyond clinking crystal in the elegant dining quarter to the open-air observation car, girded by gleaming brass rails, where your windswept hair surrenders to the steaming jungle. During a twilit blur of stilted kampongs, you find the parlor car to gape at the dexterous balance of a Thai dancer, whose golden crown mimics the splendid royal wats awaiting in Bangkok. Knowing you'll awake to a lavish breakfast tray, you succumb at last to the syncopated rhythms lulling your one-track mind toward dreamland, the next station beyond the night's wailing locomotive whistle.

Gazing Inside

the Great Australian

The world's largest living organism is a 1,200-mile-long Pacific phenomenon off the eastern coast of the Australian continent. Here billions of marine polyps are continually forming architectural walls of ever-climbing coral skeleton. You journey to Lizard Island, part of this great barrier reef. Its intricate braiding of shoals, cays, and isles has created submerged tropical gardens that sway with the waves like patches of flowers in a determined breeze. Climb to the granitic summit of Cook's Look for a champagne breakfast on the very spot from which that 18th-century explorer surveyed a hidden maze of suboceanic obstacles. At your feet in all directions, sugary beaches sweeten hidden coves of gin-clear water. Postponing that glass-bottomed boat trip, you unleash a motorized dinghy from the exclusive dock at your resort and claim a deserted inlet, shipwrecking yourself with flippers and snorkel gear. Peer through your dive mask into the silent, kaleidoscopic wonderland of a neon-brilliant fish bowl. Clouds of minnows busily explore brain-shaped limestone colonies, while giant iridescent clams appear to smack their lips at red emperors and blue-ringed octopus. Farther offshore, float into the Cod Hole, where a half-ton marlin and a score of panhandling six-foot-long potato cod nibble your extremities, swiftly numbing any concerns about encircling moray eels.

Reef

Gorilla Tracking Through the
Rain Forests of Uganda

In the heart of Africa and on the edge of extinction, a scattering of mountain gorillas cling to their shrinking cloud-soaked living quarters. At Bwindi Impenetrable National Park, an elegant wilderness camp's lantern-lit dinner is served, while on the ridges great apes construct their evening nests. Armed with a coveted tracking permit, you set out at daybreak led by a sharp-eyed jungle sleuth, who carves a bushwhacking swath through dense equatorial rain forest. Dopplerized howls of distant chimpanzees swinging across the canopy seem to haunt even the insects, as mercurial butterflies splash iridescence into dark, moss-carpeted recesses. Forge past bronze pools, avoiding a stream of hungry army ants, then with heavy gloves to thwart stinging nettles, grasp handrails of vine and lower yourself into deep, machete-hacked ravines and down the ladder of primate evolution. Telltale dung and squashed vegetation promise a rapidly approaching rendezvous. Suddenly, emerging from thick brush is the patent leather complexion of a quarter-ton silverback snacking on bitter wild celery. Avert your eyes, crouch submissively, and belch grunts of contentment. His camouflaged harem and offspring emerge to continue their buffet, until, in a King Kong–style ascent, he hoists that astonishing weight into the treetops, signaling the rest of the gorillas in the mist that naptime has begun.

Buddhist Reincarnations
Along Burma's Irrawaddy

Born in the Himalayas' melting snows, the Irrawaddy pulses through
eternally shifting sandbars, slicing Burmese paddies where ibis nit pick at
lunch. Aboard a posh waterborne lodge, you gaze upon villagers retreating to
the shade of rustling tamarinds while afternoon rays burnish gilded spires
popping out of tawny fields of sesame. Ahead, Mandalay is chockablock with
meditation centers and nipple-shaped stupas that milk your attention amidst
bonging temple gongs and chow lines of saffron-robed monks seeking
handouts. Across the way, gandy dancers muscle sledgehammers atop sheets
of gold leaf to be reverently applied as skin care treatment for enshrined
deities. At the market, merchants in sarongs and cheroot-puffing hill
tribeswomen dicker with vendors whose faces are chalked with sandalwood
paste. On the river again, you spot bamboo rafts gliding past teak-laden water
buffalo. At Pagan, you hail a clip-clopping cart for a creaky saunter through
a thousands-thick forest of topes and temples. Climb up Shwesandaw Paya to
cheer the ruby sun plummeting over vast, parched stretches of an ochre
plain. Downstream in old Rangoon, a full-moon festival at Shwedagon Pagoda
ignites a religious fairyland. Serene Buddhas patiently await genuflecting
attention as scented offerings of jasmine garlands are lobbed heavenward,
above a crowd of shaved heads chanting for reincarnation into another world.

DIRECTORY

All information is subject to change.
Reserve or book as far ahead as you can.
All organizations are open year-round
unless noted otherwise. Consult your
physician about recommended health
precautions and vaccinations, particularly
when traveling to tropical regions.

SWIMMING WITH ANGELS IN THE POLYNESIAN LAGOONS OF BORA BORA

Hotel Sofitel Marara
B.P. Box 6
Pointe Mataira, Bora Bora
French Polynesia
Tel. 689/67–70–46 or 800/763–4835
Fax 689/67–74–03
www.accor.com

$300–$500 single or double; meal plan
$56–$81. AE, DC, MC, V. 64 bungalows.
Shark-feeding excursion on glass-bottom
boat departs from hotel daily; $45 per
person; $65 per person includes lunch
on private island. Shark visibility may
be lower during Nov. rainy season.

SHINTO MAGIC IN THE TRADITIONAL JAPAN ALPS

Japan National Tourist Organization
1 Rockefeller Center, Ste. 1250
New York, NY 10020
Tel. 212/757–5640
Fax 212/307–6754
E-mail: jntonyc@interport.net
www.jnto.go.jp

JNTO provides list of minshukus but does
not make reservations. Book 1 yr in
advance. Most minshuku proprietors do
not speak English.

Festival of Asia
400 Spear St., Ste. 101
San Francisco, CA 94105
Tel. 800/880–2742
Fax 415/908–6996
E-mail tour@festivalofasia.com

12-day Takayama Festival tours Apr.
and Oct. Land costs $4,755 per person
(minimum 2 persons); single supplement
$429. AE, D, MC, V, personal check.
Festival Apr. 14 and 15, Oct. 9 and 10.

Furusato Minshuku
Ogimachi; Shirakawa-mura
Ohno-gun, Gifu-Pref.
001–56 Japan
Tel. 81/5/769/6–1033

About $55 per person, per night; includes
2 meals; excludes $2 heating fee in winter.
4 rooms.

CAMPING WITH BEDOUINS IN JORDAN'S DESERT KINGDOM

Royal Jordanian Tour Desk
6 E. 43rd St., 27th floor
New York, NY 10017
Tel. 212/949–0070 or 800/758–6876
Fax 212/949–0488

Royal Tours
Amman City Terminal/7th Circle
Box 815433
Amman, Jordan
Tel. 962/6/585–7210 or 962/6/585–7154
Fax 962/6/585–6845

Custom itinerary $200–$400 per person,
per day; includes excursions, meals,
accommodations (such as Wadi Ram guest
house or camping in desert tents), plus
visits to Bedouin encampments in Wadi
Ram desert to lodge, dine, or have tea and
coffee with Bedouins or Jordan Desert
Patrol. AE, MC, V.

SAILING THE FAMILY ISLANDS ON A BAHAMAS MAILBOAT

Port Authority
Port Department
Dock Masters Office
Box N-8175
Nassau N.P., Bahamas
Tel. 242/393–1064
Fax 242/394–1240
www.bahamasnet.com

Lady Mathilda departs Nassau Wed. 7 am
and makes four stops in Family Islands
(also called Out Islands); call for exact
schedule. $70 each way. Cash only.

WRANGLE WITH GAUCHOS ACROSS THE PAMPAS OF URUGUAY

Hosteria Estancia La Calera
Almirante Harwood 6405
1150 Montevideo, Uruguay
Tel. (5982) 600–8708
Fax (5982) 800–2077
E-mail lacalera@netgate.com.uy
www.lacalera.com.uy

$64–$90 per person, per day, double
occupancy; includes meals, horseback-
riding activities, taxes. AE, DC, MC, V.
Take private car, bus, or coach from
Montevideo to Paso de los Toros; minivan
will take you from there to guest house.

SEARCHING FOR GRIZZLIES FROM A FLOATING LUMBER CAMP

Knight Inlet Lodge
8841 Driftwood Rd.
Black Creek, BC, Canada V9J 1A8
Tel. 250/337–1953
Fax 250/337–1914
E-mail grizzly@island.net
www.grizzlytours.com

4- to 8-day trips May–Oct. $1,540–$3,040
per person, double occupancy; includes

accommodations at Painter's Lodge (1 night) and Knight Inlet Lodge, meals at Knight Inlet Lodge, wildlife-viewing tours, transportation to all tours, floatplane. AE, MC, V, personal check.

THERMAL WATERS IN DOMINICA'S VALLEY OF DESOLATION

Papillote Wilderness Retreat
Box 2287 Roseau
Commonwealth of Dominica
West Indies
Tel. 767/448–2287
Fax 767/448–2285
E-mail papillote@cwdom.dm
www.papillote.dm

$70–$175 per night for single, double, or suite; excludes meals. AE, D, MC, V. 1-night deposit required for confirmation. 8 rooms. Most passenger flights arrive at Melville Hall airport; taxi to Roseau $18. Transport can be rented in Roseau, or take local bus ($2) up mountain to Papillote. Guided day hike to Valley of Desolation and Boiling Lake can be arranged by Papillote upon arrival; $45 per day, per person; $199 for 3 days; $325 for 5 days.

THROUGH A MAZE OF ETHIOPIAN WORSHIP

Ethiopian Tourism Commission
Box 2183
Addis Ababa, Ethiopia
Tel. 251/1/150609, 251/1/513962, or 251/1/517470
Fax 251/1/513899

Ethiopian Airlines
Tel. 212/867–0095

Fun Safaris
Box 178
Bloomingdale, IL 60108
Tel. 630/893–2545 or 800/323–8020
Fax 630/529–9769

E-mail gowildnow@aol.com
www.funsafaris.com

7- to 13-day itineraries. $3,900–$6,500 per person from Washington, DC; includes international airfare, airfare within Ethiopia, accommodations, meals, guides. MC, V, personal check. Rainy season June–Sept.; heaviest rainfall July and Aug.

HIKING THROUGH THE INCAN UNIVERSE TO MACHU PICCHU

Mountain Travel Sobek
6420 Fairmount Ave.
El Cerrito, CA 94530
Tel. 510/527–8100 or 888/687–6235
Fax 510/525–7710
E-mail info@mtsobek.com
www.mtsobek.com

10- to 13-day adventure treks. $1,995–$2,895 per person, double occupancy; single supplement $450–$550; includes meals, accommodations, expert leadership, ground transportation, airport transfers; excludes airfare. AE, MC, V, personal check. Summer trips fill quickly.

Machu Picchu Hotel
Aguas Calientes, Peru
Tel. 51/84/21–1032
Cuzco reservations: Procuradores 48, Cuzco
Tel. 51/84/23–2161
Fax 51/84/22–3769

From $100 double occupancy. AE, MC, V. 26 rooms.

IN THE IRISH MISTS OF ST. PATRICK'S DOMAIN

Ashford Castle Hotel & Country Estate
Cong, Co. Mayo, Ireland
Tel. 353/92–46003
Fax 353/92–46260
E-mail ashford@ashford.ie

Reservations:
Box 28966
Atlanta, GA 30358-0966
Tel. 770/612–1701 or 800/346–7007
Fax 770/612–1725
E-mail oriordan@mindspring.com

$94–$368 double occupancy. AE, DC, MC, V. 83 rooms, 2 restaurants (jacket and tie required in evening). Rent car at Shannon Airport; 90-min drive to Ashford Castle. St. Patrick's pilgrimage last Sun. in July; from Ashford Castle drive 45 min to Croagh Patrick; 3- to 5-hr climb; bring water, and wear hiking shoes.

HEADHUNTER HOSPITALITY IN THE HEART OF BORNEO

CPH Travel Agencies
(Sarawak) Sdn. Bhd.
70 Padungan Rd.
93100 Kuching, Sarawak, Malaysia
Tel. 60/82/243708
Fax 60/82/424587
E-mail cphtrvl@pojaring.my
www.cphtravel.com.my/cph

2- to 4-day Skrang River Safari tours. $90–$200 per person (minimum 2 persons); includes longboat journey, longhouse visits, longhouse and guest-house accommodations, meals. All services have English-speaking guide.

TO THE NORTH POLE BY ICEBREAKER

Quark Expeditions
980 Post Rd.
Darien, CT 06820
Tel. 203/656–0499 or 800/356–5699
Fax 203/655–6623
E-mail quarkexpeditions@compuserve.com
www.quark-expeditions.com

17-day expeditions to North Pole July and Aug. $18,950–$23,950; includes voyage aboard *Sovietskiy Soyuz*, accommodations, meals aboard ship, helicopter and shore excursions, lectures; excludes airfare. AE, MC, V accepted for 25% deposit; balance by personal check.

BARGING BICYCLES THROUGH HOLLAND'S TULIP PLAYGROUND

Cycletours Holland
Keizersgracht 181
NL-1016 Amsterdam
Tel. 31/20/627–40–98
Fax 31/20/627–90–32
E-mail cyclefun@cycletours.nl
www.cycletours.nl

1-week Northern route/Bike and Boat Holiday tours offered Apr.–Oct. $460–$515 per person; includes barge accommodations, meals, 21-speed bicycle, guide. MC, personal check. Tulip season Apr. and May. Children's rates available.

THE DRAMA OF A SERENGETI SAFARI

Micato Safaris
15 W. 26th St.
New York, NY 10010
Tel. 212/545–7111 or 800/642–2861
Fax 212/545–8297
E-mail micatony@aol.com

17-day Stanley Wing Safari. Land arrangements $4,195–$4,995 per person, double occupancy; single supplement $875; includes meals, accommodations, flights within Africa, airport transfers, guided tours. Personal check.

Mountain Lodge Treetop Hotel
Box 123
Kiganjo-Nyeri, Kenya
Tel. 254/171–4248

$199–$360 per night for single, double, or suite; includes meals. All rooms have private balconies overlooking a floodlit water hole that animals visit at night. V.

WANDERING A SWISS FAIRY TALE

Hotel Meisser
Dorf Str. 42
7545 Guarda, Engadin
Tel. 41/81/862–21–32
Fax 41/81/862–24–80
E-mail meisser@mirus.ch
www.tourismus.ch/tour/meissguard.html

$98–$110 per person; includes dinner and buffet breakfast. AE, MC, V, personal check. 32 rooms. Guides for hikes can be arranged by hotel or with Swiss National Park for 20fr per person, per day. Public bus runs 5 times daily from Guarda train station to hotel; or call ahead to arrange pickup.

To explore the Leitern, take train to Leuk (3½ hrs from Zurich and Milan) and bus to Leukerbad. Hike to Albinen and stay at Berghotel (tel. 41/27/473–1288). Best travel time June–mid-Oct.

VOODOO CULTURE ON THE EDGE OF THE AMAZON BASIN

Movement for Eco-Tourism in Surinam (METS)
c/o Surinam Airways
5775 Blue Lagoon Dr., Ste. 190
Miami, FL 33126
Tel. 305/262–9922 or 800/327–6864
Fax 305/261–0884
E-mail mets@sr.net
www.surinfo.org/mets

4- to 5-day Gran Rio Tour. From $395; excludes airfare. Cashier's check or money order. Bring flashlight, bug repellent, raincoat, long-sleeve shirt.

TRAILING IN THE FOOTSTEPS OF TRANSYLVANIA'S DRACULA

Romania Tourist Information Office
14 E. 38th St., 12th floor
New York, NY 10016
Tel. 212/545–8484
Fax 212/251–0421

Quest Tours and Adventures
1 World Trade Center
121 SW Salmon, Ste. 1100
Portland, OR 97204
Tel. 800/621–8687
Fax 503/777–0224
E-mail tour@teleport.com
www.romtour.com/~tour

5- to 9-day Dracula tours for individuals and groups. $636– $1,760; excludes airfare. Halloween special $385–$725 per person for groups of 15 or more; includes stay at Dracula Castle Hotel. Personal check. Avoid travel in winter: roads are winding and can be dangerous.

Dracula Castle Hotel
4445 Piatra Fântânele
Jud. Bistriţa Nâsâud
Romania
Tel. 40/63/26–68–41
Fax 40/63/26–61–19

$26 single, $38 double, $66 suite. Cash. 67 rooms.

SPIRITUAL TRANCES IN A BALINESE PARADISE

Four Seasons Resort (Bali at Jimbaran Bay)
Jimbaran, Denpasar
Bali, Indonesia 80361
Tel. 62–361/701010
Fax 62–361/701020

4- to 10-night packages, 2 nights minimum. $395–$2,400 per night, double occupancy. AE, MC, V. 147 villas. 15 min

from Ngurah Rai International Airport.
Concierge arranges English-speaking
guide and car; $20 half day, $40 full day.

LIFTING THE VEIL OF MOROCCAN CASBAHS

Palais Jamai
Bab-Guissa
Fez, Morocco
Tel. 212/5/635−090
Fax 212/5/635−096

$115−$200 double occupancy. AE, MC, V.
135 rooms. Concierge arranges guides for
medina (casbah); $12 half day, $15 full
day.

La Mamounia
Ave. Bab Jdid
Marrakech, Morocco
Tel. 212/4/44−89−81
Fax 212/4/44−49−40

$190−$320 double occupancy. AE, DC,
MC, V. 171 rooms, 57 suites, 3 villas.
Concierge arranges guides for casbah; $16
half day, $27 full day.

DUGOUT EXPEDITION TO VENEZUELA'S ANGEL FALLS

Servitours, Inc.
800 Brickell Ave., Ste. 101
Miami, FL 33131
Tel. 305/381−9026 or 800/337−5292
Fax 305/577−8291

Canaima package $770−$1,269 per
person for 1- to 2-night stay; includes
airfare from Miami or New York, camp
accommodations, all meals, curiara lagoon
ride, DC-3 flight (weather permitting) over
Angel Falls; optional overnight excursion
to base of Angel Falls by dugout canoe for
additional $180 per person. AE, D,
personal check.

Canaima Camp
Av. Universidad, Torre El Chorro,
Esquina El Chorro, Piso 13
Caracas, Venezuela
Tel. 58/2/562−3022, U.S. reservations
800/428−3672
Fax 58/2/562−3475

$344 per night and $491 for 2 nights per
person, double occupancy. AE, D.
Cabanas accommodate 160 persons.

STEAMING IN LAPLAND'S CRYSTAL WILDERNESS

Finnish Tourist Board
655 3rd Ave.
New York, NY 10017
Tel. 212/885−9700 or 800/346−4636
Fax 212/885−9710
www.mek.fi

Lapland Travel, Ltd.
Koskikatu 1
Box 8156
Fin-96101, Rovaniemi
Tel. 358/16/312−622 or 358/16/346−052
Fax 358/16/312−743

Packages include Santa Claus Village and
Happy Island. Happy Island $280 per
person, per night, double occupancy;
includes accommodations, dinner at
teepee restaurant, breakfast, sauna, Arctic
Circle Ceremony, reindeer farm and
sightseeing with guide, arrival/departure
transfers. MC, V.

RAJASTHANI HALLUCINATIONS ACROSS A MAHARAJA WONDERLAND

Government of India Tourist Office
1270 Ave. of the Americas
New York, NY 10020
Tel. 212/586−4901
Fax 212/582−3274
E-mail goitony@tourindia.com
www.tourindia.com

Shiv Niwas Palace
City Palace, Udaipur
Rajasthan, India
Tel. 91/294/528−016
Fax 91/294/528−006

$125−$600 double occupancy. AE, MC, V.
34 rooms.

Lake Palace Hotel
Pichola Lake
Udaipur 313 001
Rajasthan, India
Tel. 91/294/527−961
Fax 91/294/527−974

$140−$550 double occupancy. AE, MC, V.
81 rooms.

Both hotels are on Pichola Lake. Shiv
Niwas Palace, 25 km from Udaipur
Airport, can be reached by car or taxi.
Lake Palace, 26 km from airport, is in
lake and accessible by private
complimentary boat service. Shuttle boat
service between hotels. Hire car to
Pushkar Camel Fair (Nov.), 4 hrs from
Udaipur and 11 km from Ajmer. Book
accommodations in advance. Monsoon
months July−Sept.; best travel time Oct.−
Mar.

SEEKING MOUNTAIN TRIBES IN PAPUA NEW GUINEA

Trans Niugini Tours
408 E. Islay
Santa Barbara, CA 93101
Tel. 805/569−0558
Fax 805/569−0558
E-mail mgreg@aol.com

7- to 14-day tours. Land rates $1,720−
$3,898; excludes flights within New
Guinea. Personal check. Arrive Port
Moresby and fly to Madang or Tari,
depending on itinerary.

Ambua Lodge
P.O. Box 371
Mount Hagen
Papua New Guinea
Tel. 675/542–1438
Fax 675/542–2470
E-mail pn086@tcsp.com

$275–$340 per person; includes accommodations, meals, tours, and airport transfers. AE, DC, MC, V.

A MAURITIAN CARNIVAL OF CULTURES

Air Mauritius
560 Sylvan Ave.
Englewood, NJ 07632
Tel. 201/871–8382
Fax 201/871–6983
E-mail airmkusa@concentric.net
www.airmauritius.com

7-night packages from New York start at $2,000; includes airfare and land travel. AE, personal check. Best times to travel Oct., Nov., Mar.–May.

Royal Palm
Grand Baie
Mauritius
Tel. 263–83–53
Fax 263–84–55

$350–$500 double occupancy. AE, DC, MC, V. 72 rooms, 12 suites.

THE ICY FRONTIERS OF EXTRATERRESTRIAL ANTARCTICA

Abercrombie & Kent International, Inc.
1520 Kensington Rd.
Oak Brook, IL 60521
Tel. 630/954–2944 or 800/323–7308
Fax 630/954–3324
E-mail info@abercrombiekent.com
www.abercrombiekent.com

14- to 19-day expeditions to Antarctica Nov.–Feb. $5,995–$16,995 per person, double occupancy; includes accommodations, meals, shore excursions, lectures; excludes airfare. AE, D, MC, V, personal check. Optional excursions to South Georgia and Falkland islands.

RIDING MALAY RAILS ON THE EASTERN AND ORIENTAL EXPRESS

Eastern and Oriental Express
Orient-Express Hotels, Trains & Cruises
c/o Abercrombie & Kent
1520 Kensington Rd.
Oak Brook, IL 60521
Tel. 800/524–2420
Fax 630/954–3324
E-mail info@abercrombiekent.com
www.abercrombiekent.com

2-night train packages. $1,300–3,600 per person; includes trishaw tour of Penang, boat excursion on River Kwai; excludes airfare. AE, D, MC, V.

GAZING INSIDE THE GREAT AUSTRALIAN REEF

Lizard Island Lodge
Lizard Island, P.M.B. 40
Cairns, Queensland, Australia 4870
Tel. 61/7/4060–3999, U.S. reservations 800/624–3524
Fax 61/7/4060–3991
www.qttc.com.au/pfm/acmpvrs/0008980/main.htm

$778–$929 per room, per night, double occupancy; includes meals. AE, DC, MC, V. 40 rooms. Qantas flies to Cairns; air transfers from Cairns to Lizard Island (55 min) for additional cost. Best travel time Sept.–Nov. Resort arranges dive packages that include Cod Hole.

GORILLA TRACKING THROUGH THE RAIN FORESTS OF UGANDA

Natural Habitat Adventures
2945 Center Green Ct. S, Ste. H
Boulder, CO 80301

Tel. 303/449–3711 or 800/543–8917
Fax 303/449–3712
E-mail nathab@worldnet.att.net
www.nathab.com

11-day Primate Watch adventures Feb. and May–Aug. From $4,995; single supplement $395; includes accommodations, meals, visits to chimp sites; excludes airfare. AE, D, MC, V, personal check. Long rains fall Apr.–mid-May.

BUDDHIST REINCARNATIONS ALONG BURMA'S IRRAWADDY

Road to Mandalay
Orient-Express Hotels, Trains & Cruises
c/o Abercrombie & Kent
1520 Kensington Rd.
Oak Brook, IL 60521
Tel. 800/524–2420
Fax 630/954–3324
E-mail info@abercrombiekent.com
www.abercrombiekent.com

3- to 8-night land/cruise packages. $1,590–$6,080 per person; includes meals, accommodations, flights within Burma, sightseeing excursions; excludes airfare. AE, D, MC, V.